Dichotomies
for
Dyads

A Handbook for Recognizing and Resolving Personality Conflicts in Relationships

Mark S. Majors, PhD

PRINTED IN THE UNITED STATES OF AMERICA

Published by Handbook Press

Cover/Book Design: Kris Kiler Marketing Design

International Standard Book Number: 978-0-9821249-0-1

Dedicated to all who suffer
at the hands of misattribution and confusion.
And
To the One who accepts us just as we are.

Contents

Preface

In my private practice as a counselor I commonly
find individuals who are confused about the
strain that they experience in their relationships
with others *(Dyads- any two individuals interacting
with each other)*. I have used the *Dichotomies (opposite ends of personality elements)* of psychological
type to help them to understand and reduce that
strain and discomfort. It is wonderful to see the
peace that they find when it is recognized that
neither they nor the other parties are flawed or
broken. Subsequently, I have come to the conclu-
sion that much of what is called *personality conflict*
is nothing more than a lack of knowledge and a
developed misattribution regarding the behavior
and intent of others. This text is an attempt to
put a small portion of what I have learned into a
form that will help free others from the painful
bondage of continuing conflict stemming from

naturally occurring personality differences. It is based upon the simple premise that the truth, about others, and ourselves sets us free from the pain of misattribution and rejection.

Introduction

Abigail and Lillian:
A Story Across the Sands of Time

Once upon a time there were two girls playing in a sandbox. Abigail and Lillian were seven years old and had both just moved into the new neighborhood. They were excited at the expectations that come from finding someone new to play with. Abigail sat down in the sandbox and with a shovel began very quietly and carefully piling up sand. She softly began to hum, and to mold the sand into an image that was coming to her mind. She said, "This is the shape of the mountains we visited on vacation last summer."

All of a sudden, Lillian began to take her feet and push the sand as if she were pretending to be a giant earth-moving machine. She loudly hollered "Whoosh! Whoosh!" as the waves of sand crashed over Abigail's mountains. Startled by the behavior, Abigail cried out "No, Lillian! You are ruining my mountains!"

Responding to Abigail, Lillian said, "I'm playing." She repeatedly pushed the waves over the mountains, flinging sand into the air as she yelled "Whoosh! Whoosh!"

Abigail, on the verge of tears, said, "I thought you wanted to be my friend. You have ruined my mountains," and she got up and ran home. Lillian sat stunned and confused. Her older brother, Benjamin, who had been playing off at a distance, heard the commotion and came over. Lillian looked up at Benjamin and declared "Abigail doesn't like me. We were playing vacation, so I pretended I was making the waves we saw at the beach last summer, and I guess that made her sad and now she doesn't want to be my friend."

***

All of us can relate to the story of Abigail and Lillian. We do or say things just as we have always done, or in the manner that seems natural to us, and someone around us responds with offense or hurt. Then we wonder, "Why has this happened?" Our response may focus upon either "what is wrong with them" or "what have I done wrong?" At the root of this issue is the truth that we are each unique as attested to by the patterns of our fingerprints as well as the iris of the eye, and our very DNA (except for identical twins). This includes aspects of our mannerisms and personality. There are, however, common factors or common personality elements by which we may be sorted into meaningful groups. These points of commonality are based on patterns in our culture and environment, as well as upon natural tendencies and preferences. One of the more meaningful methods of identifying these common factors is referred to as psychological type. These naturally occurring differences in psychology allow us to group individuals based upon behaviors that extend from preferred ways of being and interacting with the world around us. *Dichotomies for Dyads* is an introduction into the use of elements of psychological type differences (*Dichotomies*) to reveal and diffuse the tension and strain that may be found between two individuals (*Dyads*). In the playground Dyad of Abigail and Lillian, it was the differences on the Dichotomies of personality type that were misunderstood and resulted in the painful exchange.

An Overview of Psychological Type

Each of the individuals who are reading this text will have a different level of understanding of the concept of psychological type. Therefore, it is important to provide a brief overview of psychological type and the four naturally occurring dichotomous dimensions that are represented in this personality schema. It will not be the focus of this text to provide a deep or detailed understanding of the 16 personality types or an education into what is referred to as type dynamics. To gain a better understanding of personality type there are many texts available (*The 16 Personality Types* by Linda V. Berens and Dario Nardi). It must be noted that these four dimensions (dichotomies) do not represent all of the individual differences that can be the cause of misunderstandings or conflicts. They do, however, represent some of the common contexts that are found to be the instigating factors of misattribution and the subsequent discomfort that results.

A Short History of the Psychological Type Code

In 1921 C. J. Jung presented his theory of psychological types. He described a theory of innate psychological characteristics that were expressed in everyday thought and actions. The variation in human behavior is from basic and observable differences in mental preferences for gathering and processing information. Various combinations of these characteristics form a good portion of the expressed essence of *who* we are, and have become known as psychological type code.

> *"The idiosyncrasy of an individual is not to be understood as any strangeness in his substance or in his components, but rather as a unique combination, or gradual differentiation, of functions and faculties which in themselves are universal. Every human face has a nose, two eyes, etc., but these universal factors are variable, and it is this variability, which makes individual peculiarities possible. Individuation, therefore, can only mean a process of psychological development that fulfills the individual qualities given; in other words, it is a process by which a man*

becomes the definite, unique being that he in fact is." (Jung, 1966)

Isabel Briggs Myers began working on the first legitimate measure of Jungian psychological type in 1942 (Myers Briggs Type Indicator®; MBTI®). Myers' mother Katharine Briggs had inspired her to a passionate interest in personality type after she discovered that Jung's typology (Jung, 1923) fit well with her own observations of people around her. In reading Jung's theory they concluded that there were four dichotomous psychological dimensions:

- *Attitude (Energizing)* is the focus of attention and the direction of the source of psychological energy. The two directions of focus and energy are Extraversion and Introversion.
- *Perception (Attending)* is the mental process by which one takes in or attends to information about physical surroundings and concepts. The two forms of perception are Sensing and iNtuiting.
- *Judgment (Deciding)* is the mental process of forming decisions about the perceived information that is gathered. The two forms of judgment are Thinking and Feeling.
- *Orientation (Living)* is the preferred mental process used or lifestyle adopted for dealing with the outside world. The two methods of orientation correspond to the mental

functions of Judgment and Perception (Jung implied the preference for orientation of the mental functions and Myers accurately presented it as a necessary scale to establish the type pattern).

Based on interpretations of Jung, all four of these dimensions are thought to be dichotomous. Jung believed that people would tend to develop one preference on the scale at the expense of the other (e.g. Extraversion over Introversion). To Myers and Briggs this meant that there was a need to construct a test that was accurate in indicating which ends of the dichotomous dimensions were preferred by the individual. Most tests of psychological attributes measure how much of something a person has. Myers chose to call her measure an indicator to differentiate it from those other psychological tests and to reduce the likelihood that it would be seen as a measure of dysfunction or pathology. Therefore, the result of measuring Jungian psychological type is a four-letter code based on the person's preference for one end of each of the four dichotomous scales, not a series of numbers that represent how much of a given characteristic that is possessed by the individual. The four-letter code method provides 16 possible combinations of dichotomous results, which represent a whole type pattern (see table one).

Table one: The Sixteen Types

ISTJ	ISFJ	INFJ	INTJ
ISTP	ISFP	INFP	INTP
ESTP	ESFP	ENFP	ENTP
ESTJ	ESFJ	ENFJ	ENTJ

In 2001 a new and powerful method of measuring the psychological type dichotomies was developed. The Majors PTI® (Personality Type Inventory) uses innovative methods to accurately arrive at the 16-Type four-letter code (Table one above). Using the results from the PTI, along with the self-discovery process that occurs in professional feedback sessions, will facilitate the accurate application of the information and interventions found in this text.

Some Very Important Additions To Personality Type

There are many forms of personality typology, because there are many elements in the composition of one's personality. As mentioned earlier, the form of typology used for the discussion in this text is based upon the work of Carl G. Jung, Katherine Briggs and Isobel Myers. There have been parallel and additional expansions of the

Jungian theory by David Kiersey and Linda V. Berens. While Jung's work focused upon the belief that personality could be grouped into meaningful innate categories, Linda Berens has expanded upon the simple notion of type and the dichotomies by describing three important aspects of the self which describe the common range of variation in using one end of a dichotomy or the other (and frequently both). Description below:

CONTEXTUAL SELF
DEVELOPED SELF
CORE SELF
ADAPT AND GROW
CURRENT BEHAVIOR

The Contextual Self
The contextual self is who we are in any given environment. It is how we behave depending on what the situation requires.

The Developed Self
When our contextual behaviors become habitual and ongoing, they become an aspect of the developed self. Several factors influence our development.

The Core Self
An aspect of our personality exists from the beginning of our lives. This aspect of ourselves is in our genes, our DNA.

While the theoretical notions of Jungian personality typology are considered innate complexes, which provide elegant descriptions of human experience, *Dichotomies for Dyads* will simply describe common clashes and challenges between individuals whose preferences lie on opposite ends of a dichotomy regardless of which levels of self (contextual, developed and core) are being expressed. Further, this text presents ways of helping ourselves and others to reframe their thinking about issues in dyad relationships, without sacrificing personal beliefs or their own sense of self.

Friction can and does result from clashes of the dichotomous opposites even when the preference for a particular polar end is purely contextual. Therefore, the focus herein will remain simply upon identifying and lowering tension based upon typological misunderstandings. Increasing our knowledge of personalities improves our ability to understand others and ourselves. When we add to our understanding it promotes our acceptance of others, and acceptance is a powerful key to developing meaningful relationships. Knowledge of the Dichotomies promotes a Dyad of mutual acceptance. Acceptance helps each one of us to experience internal and external peace. Above all else, the intent of this text is to facilitate peace in our lives.

The Four Dichotomies of Psychological Type

In this portion of the text a brief description of the content of each of the four dichotomies will be presented. It is important to keep in mind that we may enjoy and participate in behaviors and activities on both ends of a dichotomy. It is our innate preference for one end of the dichotomy over the other that tends to lead us to experience one of the polar ends as more comfortable than the other. We are not limited by this truth. We can do whatever we choose. Psychological type dichotomies merely explain the common patterns of human behavior.

E/I: Energy Acquisition and Distribution

External ⟵⟶ **Internal**

The first dichotomy to be described contains the polar ends of Extraversion and Introversion. These terms represent the preference for the external or internal acquisition and distribution of psychological energy.

What is psychological energy?

We all have activities that we prefer to engage in. Some of these preferred activities stimulate increases in the thoughts and feelings of excitement, pleasure and well-being or peace. Conversely, there are activities that reduce or deplete our sense of excitement, pleasure and well-being/peace. These non-preferred activities may result in the experiences of frustration, boredom, and irritation. These non-preferred activities should not be confused with the experiences such as going to the dentist or hitting one's hand with a hammer while attempting to drive a nail -- most individuals would consider such activities as painful regardless of preference for Extraversion or Introversion. Rather, this refers to everyday work and leisure activities like reading, speaking to groups, being physically active, or mentally busy.
For example, being inside reading a book, or quietly doing a craft on a rainy day may give great joy and peace to those preferring internal energy acquisition and distribution. Yet, this

may (after a short time) leave those preferring external energy sources experiencing the need to go somewhere to interact more directly and physically with individuals or the environment (e.g. the mall or a gym). When psychological energy is getting low the experience is the same for both those preferring Extraversion or Introversion; lower mood, agitation, irritability and frustration are common. A lively company meeting may charge the psychological battery of those preferring external acquisition and distribution of energy, but may result in a need to be quiet and/or alone for the "now drained" individuals preferring internal acquisition.

Thinking about this energy in terms of the simple battery illustration above can help in understanding this concept. Being charged up with psychological energy is joyful, while being discharged is not. Electrical things work well with charged batteries, and work less well or stop when batteries are becoming discharged or running down.

This concept of psychological energy should not be confused with becoming sleepy or physically tired. We all need daily rest and sleep. Psychological energy is a mental energy resource that facilitates action (externally or internally) that is necessary and desired in life. It is the direction or orientation of the source of energy that is reflected in the preference that is expressed. The dichotomy of psychological energy has the opposite ends of Introversion and Extraversion.

External | The preference for External acquisition and distribution of *psychological energy*

Individuals who have a preference toward the extraversion end of this dichotomy will receive energy from and direct energy to the outer world. External energy will be most commonly expressed by action and interaction. They will tend to process their lives through verbal statements and discussion. They enjoy going and doing, often seeking out action and activities that involve conversation and connecting. Although comfortable thinking quietly and reflecting, these non-external tasks will tend to be accomplished in shorter bursts, interspersed by the motivation to participate in the external environment. Their robust desire to interact can be viewed as irritating and intrusive to the internal that is trying to collect their thoughts and reflect (charge their battery).

| Internal | The preference for Internal acquisition and distribution of *psychological energy* |

Those who have a preference for introversion will choose to restrict or moderate their connection with the external environment in order to facilitate the reflective contemplation that provides the source of their psychological energy. While no less appreciative of human interaction than their external opposites, they may display the preference for more quiet and less crowded interpersonal experiences, which leave adequate pause for contemplative thought to facilitate and engage in the interaction. With the internal preference, the stimulation from the external world is manifested in the energizing reflective thought of or about the experiences of life. The internal exchange of energy is most efficiently done through interactions and environments that enable the freedom to be reflective before the commitment of action. Those preferring Extraversion and who are eager-to-engage may experience the quiet deliberate pace of the individual preferring Introversion as representing an aloof attitude or as an expression of disinterest.

S/N: Method for Information Perception

Sensing ⟵————————————⟶ **iNtuiting**

   Perception contains the dichotomous preferences of Sensing and iNtuiting. These preferences
underlie the functional processes that occur when
we attend to sensory information (current or
from memory) originating from the surrounding
physical world. We all take in information from
our environment through the five natural senses.
We see, hear, smell, taste, and touch the surrounding world and will subsequently have memories
of those sensory experiences. What we see is the
same for all of us until it enters this processing
function. Here is where the dichotomy results.
There is an automatic tendency to process the
sensory information in two basic ways.

Sensing

> The preference for
> concrete, factual *perception*

Sensing is the preference that is expressed when
the focus of the perceptive process is a pragmatic
and factual experience. Those with this preference
believe that the facts do speak for themselves
and there is seldom a need to go beyond them.
They will typically find comfort in viewing the
tried and true methods of accomplishing tasks
as a sufficient, if not necessary, course of action.

Past experiences can provide concrete foundations for answers to the questions that arise when
information is perceived. This preference may
lead the sensing preferring individual into fact-
finding forays to answer the questions of "How,
What, When, or Where?" They have a realistic
perspective that is anchored in the comfortable
foundation of pragmatism and facts. Those
who prefer the intuiting end of this dichotomy
may find it difficult to retain or present enough
concrete, detailed information to satisfy the fact-
hungry inquisitive individuals who prefer the
sensing process.

iNtuiting	The preference for abstracting possibilities in *perception*

Those who prefer iNtuiting have a perceptual
preference to look for the possibilities and relationships among the facts and their corresponding
ideas. This preference is expressed in their desire
for theoretical overviews that allow for flexibility
in interpretation and application of information.
The processing of factual information tends to
occur only to the extent that those facts possess
utility for innovation and change. Factual details
are merely elements of the connections that
form in this perception experience, and may be
overlooked or set-aside during the processing.
The "what may be" focus of these individuals
will tend to keep them engaged in future oriented

thinking. Those with the opposite sensing preferences may become frustrated with the factually
loose expressions and endless possibilities of
those who prefer iNtuiting.

T/F: Method for Judging and Deciding

Thinking ⬅————————————➡ **Feeling**

The dichotomy of making judgments or decisions involves the two preferences for using
either logical Thinking processes or relationship
and value motivated Feelings in making choices.
Everyone thinks and everyone has feelings about
thoughts and experiences. Further, we all need
to frequently make judgments and decisions
about our lives and our perceptual experiences.
Some decisions may focus upon yielding the best
outcome, while others may seek to produce what
works best for all involved. These dichotomously
differing ways of making judgments and decisions are equally valuable for balanced living. The
accuracy of the decisions that we make is important. This dichotomy represents the two different
ways of establishing what accuracy is.

Thinking

> *Judging and Deciding*
> through Logical Thought

The preference for making judgments through the process of logical thinking involves a need for logical clarity. This clarity occurs when perceptual information is objectively evaluated based upon strict logical criteria. In general this decision-making process will follow a consistent logical pattern of "if this is true, and/or this is true, then this is the best choice." The "right" thing to do is making the choice with the best outcome. Feelings or emotional interactions with the decision are seldom necessary. This is because the deciding action is a process with rules that simply weight the pros and cons to the service (support) of the outcome. Logically based values and morals are included in the decision-making process, and will sometimes dramatically alter the decisions that are made. The influence of strongly held morals and values may result in firm black and white judgments that seem unusually intense from these rather matter-of-fact individuals. The expression of emotions will rise when the joy or aggravation of the decision's accuracy is revealed. Those holding to the opposite relational feeling end of the dichotomy may view the matter-of-fact pronouncement, flowing from the decisions or judgments made by those with this logical thinking preference, as cold and heartless.

Feeling

Judging and Deciding using the
Values of Relationships and Harmony

Individuals, who have a preference for Feeling judgments and decisions, make choices based on beliefs, values, and ideals they believe will lead to greater inner and external resonance in the overall situation. They are keenly attuned to the effect of decisions on others and seek to implement decisions that enhance relationships. They often have a need to process the emotional and interpersonal consequences of decisions. Those with a preference for feeling judgments view the consensus forming process as integral to the judgments that are being made. This tendency for overtly checking with involved parties, to maintain harmony and relational stability, is central to this form of decision-making. The need to process and check with the condition of others throughout the decision-making process can be viewed, by those holding to the opposite logical decision-making preference, as an indication of personal instability and/or a wasting of time.

J/P: Method for Life Interaction/Orientation

Judging ←————————————————→ **Perception**

This dichotomy represents the method that is preferred for interacting with or orienting to life and living. It contains the polar opposite preferences of life by making decisions and judgments as opposed to life through perceptual experience. These two polar preferences represent what we see as we experience or observe one another during the process of our daily lives. This dichotomy is in essence an innate expression of the individual's mental style of living; we will prefer to "choose or experience" life. We are all able to learn to do elements of both ends of this dichotomy, but there is one that will be preferred the most.

Judging

> Life Through Making
> Decisions and Judgments

Individuals with a preference for living life through judgments and decisions enjoy planning and processing daily experiences. Comfort is experienced through the methodical organization of tasks and activities. Satisfaction is achieved as each of the day's set goals is completed. When those who prefer Judging are aware of the plans for events and activities, then they experience an assurance that the necessary tasks and goals will be finished in the allotted time. Interruptions in the plan or method can create frustration and distract these individuals. The preference to decide, act and have closure on the events of life is naturally pleasing to them. Getting an early start on an activity or task promotes a sense of well-being and peace. Frequently, the need to know the plan and steps that will occur is viewed as an indication of demanding and controlling behavior by those who hold the opposite preference of life by perception.

Perception

> Living Life with a
> Perception Orientation

The preference for living life through the process of perception is indicated when the experience of life is the desired process of life. Individuals who prefer the perceiving end of this dichotomy will tend to set the events of life in a flexible and open-ended style. For these individuals deadlines are met, but the process to achieve the goal may be expressed or unfold over time. Unscheduled interruptions are viewed as a natural part of living with little stress or concern over the resulting diversions. Changes in plans or decisions regarding processes are viewed as simply elements of the emergent style of life. They can become bored or irritated with the restrictions of rigid schedules or guidelines. The open-ended, unfolding manner in which individuals with this preference proceed in the tasks and activities of life can be viewed as chaotic and irresponsible by those holding a preference for the opposite judging way of life.

Passionate Preferences

Each of us has a fundamental need to believe that we are competent and accurate in our perception of life, and the decisions that we make regarding our lives. When our beliefs about our self-competence are questioned (either directly or indirectly), then our emotions may rise to the point of strong passion, and this may initiate a defensive response or a pattern of painful negative thoughts about our self. Therefore, if the preference we hold on one of the dichotomies is portrayed as wrong or flawed by someone holding an opposite preference on that dichotomy, we may view this as an attack upon our personal competency. It is this self or other imposed *tyranny of the dichotomous opposite* that is the foundation for the tension that rises in personality type differences. We ascribe truth and value to our way of being and may consequently choose to ascribe error (or discomfort) as the descriptor for another individual's preferred opposite choices. Simple discussions can become a defense of who we are as we mount a *passionate defense* of an erroneously constructed straw man.

Sometimes during the tension we will reconsider our own qualities as flawed and negative. This can lead to distrust or dislike of the self, a denial of who we are, and false negative beliefs about our value as an individual. When a Dyad interaction consistently leaves us hurting in our sense of self, then we will tend to withdraw or avoid the interaction. This is maladaptive (problem producing) in most of our important relationships.

Relationship Level of Value

In our opening story we saw the tension rise between Abigail and Lillian over the forms of expression in play. Abigail's subtle sand constructions and Lillian's bulldozer-like waves clashed in a painful tsunami of misinterpretation and difference. Why would there be such a high level of discomfort in a sandbox for friends? To answer this question, we will turn to a discussion of the perception of the value of dichotomous relationships.

Few would disagree with the claim that there are not many relationships more important to seven and eight year old little girls than friends to play with. The reality is that the more importance or value that is placed upon a relationship with another individual, the more discomfort that will be experienced when differences are believed to represent attack, rejection or proof of a flaw. There is a vertical relationship dimension that exists for each Dyad, which is influenced by the dichotomous dimensions of psychological type. See diagram below:

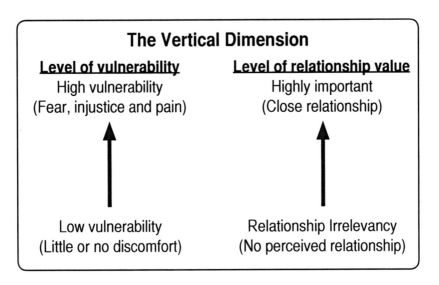

For each of the four dichotomies the level of discomfort that will be experienced through misunderstanding and misattribution is typically related to a level of vulnerability perceived by that individual. Small misattributions in highly vulnerable relationships result in higher levels of discomfort, whereas large misattributions in low vulnerable relationships may result in no discomfort. Therefore, vulnerability and the potential for discomfort may increase with the increase in value ascribed to the relationship. Because finding a new friend to play with is so important to children, Abigail's misattribution of Lillian's seashore experience was viewed as rejecting and mean. Relationships with little ascribed value are typically impotent at creating discomfort from clashing dichotomies.

Therefore, when there is misattribution resulting from dichotomous preferences, one way for the discomfort to dramatically increase is through the heightened levels of importance or value that are placed on the relationship. There is one other common factor that leads to the generation of dyad discomfort. This issue involves the vulnerability to the sense of self that a particular dichotomy preference holds for the individual. This is referred to as the ascribed special value of the dichotomy preference.

Ascribed Special Value of the Dichotomy Preference

Ron and Louie: A Story of Importance.

Ron and Louie have been working together in the shipping department for about a month. Ron had been in the shipping and receiving department for five years and Louie just transferred in from the warehouse. The transfer for Louie was seen by him as a necessity to keep working for the company because he could no longer tolerate the criticism of the warehouse supervisor. Louie believes that his previous supervisor was too fussy regarding how things were to be done, in particular, the order in which they were to be done (a preference for life by judging). His supervisor would question his ability to follow instructions or understand the protocols for storing and retrieving items in the warehouse. Louie maintained that it was the importance of the work being completed, not rigid adherence to a protocol of order that was important. He began to feel belittled by the supervisor whenever they would clash over this issue. The result was that Louie chose to transfer to escape the painful dyad relationship.

In the shipping and receiving department, Ron's leadership style involves modeling behaviors and gentle instructions. He's a quiet man, unlike Louie's supervisor from the warehouse, and doesn't use a lot of verbal cues in communication. Serious tension arose one day between Ron and Louie during the fourth week of Louie's 60-day probationary period in this new department. It seems that Ron made a simple suggestion to Louie to try a different method of processing incoming containers and Louie snapped back at Ron that he was smart enough to do this job without Ron's picky input. This preference to perform his job in a less structured more fluid manner (a preference for life by perceiving) was directly connected with the high value that he placed upon his job.

Louie, like most individuals, placed great importance/value on his job and job performance, and this in turn meant that his relationship with his new supervisor, Ron, was an important (high value) relationship. The heightened sensitivity that Louie developed with his previous supervisor in the warehouse, in combination with the differing approaches to processing materials between him and Ron, resulted in a painful misattribution of Ron's behavior and intention. Ron was surprised at Louie's comment and uncertain of where this intense emotional expression had come from within Louie. The pain from the dyad relationship with the warehouse supervisor had contaminated the new dyad relationship with Ron. Louie's passionate defense against the tyranny of the dichotomous opposite was a misattribution carryover from the old dyad.

***

Much of the time when there are differences between two individuals that reveal themselves during everyday interactions, there is little threat and little misattribution about the difference. These differences in the preferred dichotomies are typically seen as simply differences, void of special meaning, regardless of the importance or value of the relationship. Yet all of us possess elements of our personality that have more vulnerability to the threat of misattribution than others (see diagram on the next page).

Interaction of Dyad Relationship Value with Dichotomy Threat to Self

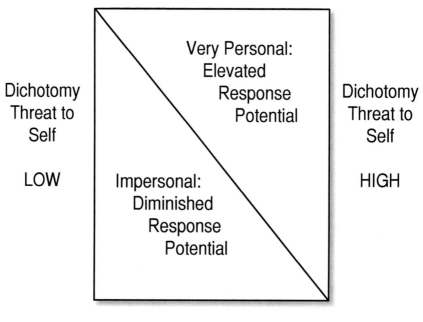

Relationship Value HIGH

Dichotomy Threat to Self

LOW

Very Personal: Elevated Response Potential

Impersonal: Diminished Response Potential

Dichotomy Threat to Self

HIGH

Relationship Value LOW

Note: As either relationship value or dichotomy threat increase, then the potential for an elevated response increases.

Some individuals who are less secure in their sense of self may find themselves vulnerable (Dichotomy Threat to Self High) across many elements of their preferred personality expression.

For example: Louie's former supervisor would make statements that resulted in Louie believing that there was something wrong with his preferred style (Perceiving) of performing tasks at work. Other individuals may seldom ever experience such a threat, because elements of their personality dichotomies are not strongly connected with their beliefs about their competence or self-image (Dichotomy Threat to Self Low). Sometimes individuals may actually see their preferred dichotomy choice as under attack even when it is completely unintended (e.g. Ron's simple suggestions). As seen in the diagram, either a high threat to self or a high relationship value can generate an elevated emotional response. The elevated emotional response may manifest in defensiveness or withdrawal from the relationship (or both). In the case of Louie, there was both high relationship value and high dichotomy threat to self.

The goal in this text is not an evaluation of the individual's sense of security but identification of potential conflicts that will arise between individuals preferring opposite poles of one of the dichotomous elements of personality type. It is possible for everyone to evaluate persistent tension in their dichotomous relationships to see if false assumptions about personality dichotomies are behind the discomfort. For the counselor or professional, patterns of misattributed threat will point to underlying issues with the sense of self that are valid points of intervention with clients.

By increasing our understanding of our own preferences for a polar end of each of the four common psychological type dimensions (dichotomies), we can depersonalize (lower) the threat to the self that occurs in the important dyad relationships that we have.

Individual differences are a beautiful expression of the tapestry of interpersonal relationships. Real attacks and threats are painful, but the common misunderstandings from misattributions that occur, because of preferred differences on psychological type dimensions, need not be a source of pain in our lives. When we understand the benign nature of the difference and are able to help others place positive attribution on our own preference, the prevalence of meaningless yet painful exchanges may be reduced or eliminated. *Dichotomies for Dyads* represents a simple revelation of the misattributions from preferred individual differences.

Dichotomies in Action: Dyad Misattributions

The remainder of this text will present information about the psychological type dichotomies within occupational and personal settings. While it may be argued that the distinction between occupational and personal settings is artificial and sometimes nonexistent, it is presented here as distinguishing between moderate importance (occupational) and strong importance (personal) relationship dyads.

The reader is encouraged to return to the detailed descriptions of the dichotomies and the passionate preferences, during the next segments on the occupational interaction and personal interaction settings. This will help to develop a useful understanding of the potential impact that may come from our misguided perceptions of importance. The examples that are provided represent only a very small portion of the possibilities for misattribution, and are intended to stimulate investigative thought about the dichotomies that exist in dyads.

Occupational Relationships

Occupational relationships are an integral part of life. Some individuals tend to spend their days working alone with few meaningful dyad inter-actions and relations throughout the workday. Others have working environments that are based on consistent multiple dyadic relationships. The numbers of relationships only represent opportu-nities for clashes, not that there will necessarily be any clashes at all or that ones that do occur will be serious or important.

One feature of occupational experiences that presents a unique dyad for everyone is the dyad between the person and the occupational envi-ronment itself. Environments have their own psychological type expression. As you read the following descriptions and vignettes try to recog-nize the environment's position on the dichotomy under discussion. Keep in mind the ever-present interaction between individual and environment.

E/I: Energy Acquisition and Distribution

External ⟵————————————⟶ **Internal**

The principal area in which an E-I misattribution can result in negative influence in the work environment can be seen simply through the differing forms of activity that are found at the dichotomy ends. The type of work environment is in part a function of the tasks that are performed in a given environment and the makeup of the personalities of the individuals inhabiting that environment. Because externals will naturally acquire and distribute psychological energy through movement, interaction and activity, an external environment will tend to involve more activity and interaction. This, of course, is comfortable for externals in the Get-and-Give of their energy pattern. However, for an internal in that external environment, there is a scarcity of opportunity to internally reflect, process and think in order to acquire their necessary psychological energy. The quietness of the internal in that environment, along with the periodic irritability from energy depletion may result in externals labeling the internal as pejoratively different.

The converse is obviously true in the internal working environment where quiet, reflective tasks and activities are the norm. Multiple internals can spend their workday side by side in quiet energizing comfort. The external in this environment, in their attempt to satisfy energy acquisition and distribution needs, may be viewed as the office interruption. The process of going from person to person seeking interaction and opportunity for expression can be received with subtle rejection that may cause the external to question their choice of jobs or discredit their own reasons for needing interaction. The externals themselves may find the environment boring and unfulfilling, and at the same time be viewed by their internal co-workers as interruptive and disrespectful. The internals, and even the externals themselves in moments of self-doubt, may be thinking, "why do they need to talk so much," or "they should spend more time working and less talking."

Supervisory Interruptious

Mark had been in his new position as director of research for one week. All had been well with everyone in his new workplace. His two staff subordinates, Sandy and Elva seemed to like him and there was a healthy relationship with everyone. One day when things became busy in the office Mark went to Sandy several times to consult with her about procedures or have her do needed tasks. In the middle of the afternoon Sandy went home ill with a headache. Mark thought nothing of this and went about his day. Twice more in the next week Sandy became ill and needed to leave early due to illness. Their relationship began to show signs of strain. Mark would request work and input from Sandy, and Sandy seemed more and more put out by his frequent interactions. Mark consulted the HR staff member and with consults involving both him and Sandy discovered the problem. Sandy had a preference for Internal and Mark for External psychological energy. While Sandy is extremely competent in her duties and work ethic, she was being drained of energy by all of Mark's repeated interruptions and conversation. After a few meetings together with HR, Sandy and Mark decided on a new rule to help their interactions. Mark could interrupt Sandy in the middle of a working task once or twice with no concerns about her concentration or energy level. After three or four interruptions she may warn him if becoming confused and irritated. After that point a headache would appear and she may need to leave. Mark agreed to be careful with his need for external interaction and avoid interrupting Sandy when working on a task unless necessary.

S/N: Method for Information Perception

Sensing ◄━━━━━━━━━━━━━━━━━━━━━► iNtuiting

Workplace environments are filled with perceptive activities. Most occupational settings require the use of both ends of this dichotomy. Even so, most of those environments will be weighted to either the sensing or the intuiting end of the dichotomy. Sensing dominant environments will tend to have a fundamental need to acquire and disseminate factual and pragmatic elements of the business content. Individuals comfortable with viewing information and tasks with this orientation will experience this environment as making sense and meaningful when the facts are known and pragmatism is the rule. Individuals expressing and preferring intuitive perceptual experiences may find their contribution to the task and activities of the sensing work environment unwelcome and undervalued. The comfort with which the sensing individuals consistently operate in facts and pragmatism may be seen by the intuitive as an opportunity for change, and the sensing individuals may see the request for change as a workplace corruption.

In the dichotomously opposite situation of the intuitive environment, it is the norm to spend time and energy reviewing and musing over the possibilities. While facts are important to the intuitive, they are secondary to the exploration of "what may be." Those individuals with a preference for sensing may experience this environment as displaying a deficit in concrete processes and factual information. Prompted by the need for the practical and tangible, the sensing individual may come to the rescue armed with copious facts and detail. When this help is met with rejection it will tend to be frustrating for the "sensing at heart." The persistent fluid nature of the intuitive processing environment is comfortable for those with intuitive preference. The sensing's persistent questions and attempts to gather facts with which to function are experienced as a frequently unanswerable thorn in the side for many who prefer intuition.

It can be very challenging to understand the opposite end of the perceptual dichotomy, and Jung referred to this dichotomy as irrational. This meant that we are not easily able to move from one end to the other in our understanding or action. This truth can make understanding of this dichotomy challenging.

Stupid Moves

Sam and John were president (Sam) and executive vice president (John) of a large product supply corporation. The business had recently begun to really take off and was making very good profit.

This would lead most to believe that all was well at the top, but not in this case. After a number of very heated board meetings the HR director called in a consulting troubleshooter to stop the escalating tensions before the company was fractured and suffering financially due to conflict.

It seems that John and the rest of the board had been confrontational with Sam during a board meeting. John had led the rebellion (Sam's words) by suggesting that Sam was proposing stupid moves for the company. Sam became furious at the hostility toward his leadership and was on the verge of resigning and starting legal action to break up the business. After assessing their potential personality types using the Majors PTI, the troubleshooter sat down with Sam and John. Sam was proposing bold new changes for the company in an effort to capitalize on the new strength that had been gained. John had demanded facts and proof that the proposals would work before he would even consider them. Sam believed that considering the possibilities could be done without specifics, which could be gotten later after some preliminary decisions were made. John thought that this was the stupid part of the proposal and a waste of time. Sam had responded to John's insistence on facts by accusing him of strangling the company to death.

Sam confirmed that he had a preference for intuitive and John that he preferred sensing on the perceptive dichotomy (SN). Two years earlier John had left a company that was failing because of miscalculations in new ventures. John did not want to see this happen again. This concern resulted in a passionate expression of his sensing preference. Sam, on the other hand, believed that the company would need to act now to grow or be pushed out of emerging markets by competitors. Sam had put 20 years into this company and wanted it to be a legacy that continued to grow. Both men had high value into the discussion founded in their SN dichotomy positions. The understanding of their personality differences and simple methods of integrating both ends of this dichotomy into the board meetings without the negative labeling allowed the company to move forward with reasonable safety. Neither man changed his position; they simply stopped labeling the other in negative ways. The acceptance led to progress.

T/F: Method for Judging and Deciding

Thinking ⟵——————————————⟶ Feeling

Making judgments and decisions in the workplace environment will many times by necessity be outcome oriented. This logical linear directive to provide the best outcome and facilitate the viability and profitability of the organization promotes bottom-line logical T decision-making. While the judgment dimension is perhaps the most fluid of all the dichotomies, meaning many individuals commonly traverse to the opposite polar ends, it can quickly be the most inflammatory when the perception of a violation of outcome or relationship values is encountered. The relational harmonious feeling preferring individual in a logical thinking environment does well until the trap door of logical processing drops them out of the decision-making loop. The injured feeling type's insistence to participate and contribute to the pre-determined outcome-oriented decision is met with bewilderment and frustration by the ones preferring logical thinking who see no need for further discussion. This perceived relationship violation can wound an unsuspecting individual preferring feeling judgments who may view this as a personal affront on their sense of belonging and meaningfulness in the organization.

Conversely, the individuals with a thinking preference, finding themselves in the feeling process of consensus building decision-making, may watch in bewilderment as the outcome is marginalized for the sake of harmony and the "common good." Those preferring thinking that are unwilling to participate in the consensus process may find their proclamations of outcome-based decisions treated with scorn and rejection. Labeled as heartless and cold, many thinking preference individuals will hide in their office to avoid feeling flawed in their relationships with the feeling culture. Impatient with the process and wanting to move forward, unsuspecting folks with a thinking preference may simply want to move on.

Pass Another HR Person Please

Some occupational environments are by nature logical. Written software code is mostly an articulation of Boolean logic. Therefore, it is not difficult to understand that some companies that specialize in software development might be composed of mainly logical thinking individuals in the management structure. Frank was the manager of the development branch of a major software company. They had lost three HR directors in less than 90 days. Frustrated by the inability to keep this important staff position filled Frank asked an HR friend in another organization to help him out.

The friend called the three departed staff members and had a chat with them about their experiences with Frank and the software company. Then they had a conversation with Frank and his top management group to find out what process was used in selecting the HR person. It did not take long to figure out what was happening. One manager said that we seem to just chew them up. It's become a joke with us, "pass another

HR person please" another one said. This was a purely logical thinking group of individuals. They hired someone that would "fit in" with them, a very logical HR person. Two of the three HR persons even knew programming and functioned in Boolean logic. What was the problem?

The programming staff itself was also composed of a large majority of individuals preferring thinking, but they would come to the new HR persons with their personal problems and issues and found the experience negative. It seems that the previous HR person, who had retired, was a warm and friendly woman that was in her early 60's, and was extremely relational. All of the programming staff were used to going to her for employment issues and other advice. The new HR persons did not have time for this and quickly got tired of dealing with these relationship needs. The top managers were under the care of a central management HR individual and did not have personal experiences with the HR staffers whom they had selected.

Frank and the management team had selected a replacement for their personal comfort and interaction. The woman who was the previous HR director had often gotten after the management staff for erroneous decisions that could adversely affect morale in the company. She kept things running smoothly in the relationship department.

Frank thought that the change to a closer match would be good, or more comfortable for him.

J/P: Method for Life Interaction/Orientation

Judging ⬅——————————➡ **Perception**

Functioning in the work environment with either a perceptual or judgment orientation is often an expression of learned behaviors interwoven with the innate psychological preference. The vast majority of occupational environments function based on structure, schedule and deadlines. The "plan" can frequently become the most valued element of the organization. Environments managed by individuals preferring judging, who value the plans, schedule and structure as the dominant feature of the environment in which they lead, produce an occupational experience for some perceptive preferring individuals that resembles working in a straitjacket (restraining their normal impulses and preference to go with the flow). The perceptive preferring individual's failure to yield to the presence of the "plan" may result in their being labeled as an occupational anarchist, subverting what is believed by the judging opposites as the natural order of things. The preference for perception can be viewed by the opposite as sloppy and irresponsible. Sometimes, even those preferring

judging themselves, when faced with plan interruptions and course corrections, may temporarily
hold their occupational breath until the winds of
change cease to blow.

Conversely, the perceptual work environment
is by contrast typically driven by what is directly
in front of them, or the current pressing or
presenting issue. This will tend to require rapid
responses to changing issues. The individuals
preferring judging, finding themselves in the
rare perceptual dominated work environment,
may persistently request an answer to the question "What are we doing?" The unfolding, and
often pressure-prompted environment, may
leave their viscera in knots of confusion. They
would love to start early on a project if someone
would just give them the plan early enough.
The perceptive preferring leadership will persistently insist that those preferring judging
relax and watch the unfolding of the plan in real
time. They will not be sure why the one who
prefers judging requires knowing all things in
advance (perceived as a controlling behavior).
Despondent and disillusioned, those preferring
judging may retreat into the comfort of "Just tell
me what you want me to do." No one wants to
be perceived as rigid and inflexible.

You do it Your way, I'll do it Mine

A new discount store distribution center opened up in a small midwestern town. Kathy and June had graduated from high school together three years ago and were now going to be working alongside each other in their new jobs at the distribution center. They did not know each other very well in high school but both thought that it would be fun to start this new position together. Their job involved organizing the new stock material as it came into the center. They were given lists of various storing and organizing projects, and were to work together as a team to get the work done on time for distribution as the stores were requesting the new products.

On Friday after one week of employment Kathy went home from work mad, stating that she may not come back on Monday morning. June was not in the best spirits either and went to talk to Linda, the unit manager. Linda wanted to know what happened to June and Kathy. They had started out so happy and appeared to get along well. June told Linda that when they got their first assignment there was tension. Kathy had wanted to start the project right away, but June had wanted to do other stuff first and wait a few days to start the project. After all, it was due on Thursday and they had plenty of time. June went along with Kathy on the first project but on Wednesday of that first week another project came in that needed to be completed on the following Wednesday. The first project done and out of the way, Kathy wanted to get started on this one. June told her to lighten up, they have a week and it will only take a few hours. Kathy told June that she had not learned good work habits and that she would have to show her the ropes. June told Kathy that she was just as good a worker as her, but Kathy just wanted to be bossy; she told her, "you do it your way, I'll do it mine." By that first Friday afternoon there was a relationship meltdown.

On Monday morning Linda sat them down along with the conflict mediator from HR. The mediator told them that there was a simple personality conflict and that it can be resolved quickly. Kathy preferred Judging and June preferred Perception as methods of facing work assignments. June is energized by deadlines and Kathy finds them unnerving if the work is not done early. Neither of them knew that this difference was normal. June decided that she did not want to be the cause of Kathy's stress, and Kathy admitted that it was not necessary to get in such a big hurry. There were always things that needed to be done as part of their everyday work tasks. They reached a balance that involved June producing an estimate of how long she believed it would take to get the task done and starting halfway before that pressure time that she would normally start. This gave Kathy enough breathing room not to be afraid that the work would not be done on time. After a few weeks it seemed that this compromise and cessation of negative comments resulted in the development of a new friendship and work relationship.

Personal Relationships

The personal relationships that are discussed in this section of the text are high value relationships that carry high risk for pain and injury. Unlike the variability of occupational relationships, these always have strong meaning and high importance for our lives. The similarities with the occupational dyads are in the consistent misattribution from the dichotomies. In these relationships the misattributions can carry the special meaning of rejection.

E/I: Energy Acquisition and Distribution

External ⬅————————————➤ **Internal**

In close personal relationships the acquisition and distribution of psychological energy referred to as E and I, external and internal, presents many opportunities for conflict that are derived from misattribution and distortion. When one member of the dyad is external and the other internal, levels of expression are naturally different. When both individuals are operating with high levels of energy, it is still possible for the externally preferring to interpret the internally preferring as somehow uncomfortable or unhappy. Conversely, those with a preference for internal might interpret the external preference as intrusive and irritating. These interpretations can become acute and negative when one of the dyad's energy reserves is low.

Don't they ever shut up?

Paul and Lori were in their last year of college and about three months away from their long-awaited marriage. Paul was a reserved internal preferring person studying Engineering and Lori a very social person preferring external who was studying Marketing. One Saturday morning while at a breakfast meeting with Lori's family (two external preferring sisters, external preferring mother and dad), where wedding plans were being discussed, Paul began to withdraw more and more and after about an hour of lively interaction at the table, he leaned over to Lori and asked the question "Don't they ever shut up?" with a very negative tone in his voice.

Lori was taken aback by Paul's statement, but quickly returned to the joyful interaction with her family. Later that day Lori confronted Paul about his comments at the breakfast table. "You think there is something wrong with my family; you always complain about my friends. You just don't like anybody!"

Paul responds, "It seems like none of your family ever shut up; they go on and on just making noise."

Lori looked at him and said, "You are always trying to control me and you don't want me to have any fun."

Paul said, "Control you? That's impossible! Besides, you never just want to be with just me. There always has to be others."

In frustration, the couple went to a counselor in an attempt to salvage their relationship.

***

The relationship between Paul and Lori has a very high value for them both. Therefore, the words that were spoken out of their misattributions were particularly painful and damaging. In the initial counseling session with them both, the Extraversion and Introversion dichotomy was discussed. It was revealed that on the Saturday morning as with many times in their relationship, Paul had gone with Lori and her expressed highly energetic external interactions, only to find himself feeling frustrated and irritated after about 90 minutes. Lori had noticed the change in Paul when she was with family and friends. She had interpreted his irritation as a flaw and as a potential problem. She believed Paul was stuck-up and controlling. Paul's interpretation of Lori had been that she was self-centered and required the attention of multitudes. When Lori would spend a few hours alone with Paul she would become ancy and irritated, and then want to go do this or that. Paul would experience this as rejection and wonder why she didn't want to just spend time alone with him. After describing the nature of external and internal acquisition and distribution of energy, the couple began to laugh at their painful misattributions. When they were introduced to the concept of psychological energy management and conservation, they immediately were willing to take responsibility for the awareness of their own energy inventory. Harsh words that were accusing and rejecting were replaced with a tender vocabulary of acceptance and nurturing. Knowledge of the elements found in this dichotomy can quickly improve acceptance and harmony in close personal relationships.

Any time a psychological energy reserve becomes low and the ensuing strain and irritation emerges within the individual's thinking processes, there is an effort to place attribution for this uncomfortable experience. Often the attribution will fall upon anyone who thwarts our efforts to regain energy. When awareness of this dichotomy and its importance for mental enjoyment is understood, then conservation and management techniques can be implemented to avoid unnecessary negative low energy responses. Further, when periods of low energy do occur, it is important to halt the external projection of responsibility.

S/N: Method for Information Perception

Sensing ⬅➡ **iNtuiting**

Perception is a natural and continuous part of our existence. There is a need for the practical factual sensing to exist alongside the abstract possibilities of the intuitive. This mental function only presents challenges in personal dichotomies when the internal thoughts are verbalized or expressed in the external environment. Jung's reference to this function as irrational implied that it is more of a hard-wired response than an intentional choice. This leads to the distinct possibility that what is believed, as one's internal perceptual experience, is truly universal and common to everyone. The overt expression of opposite in this dichotomy can lead to disbelief and bewilderment. A frequent misattribution of dishonesty or deficiency is common. If you have not seen, heard, smelled, tasted, or felt what I have, then you are an idiot or liar. This can cause a strong personal relationship to reel in rejection and pain.

You're not very practical!

Claire was excited as she pulled up to the college dormitory to pick up her daughter Susan for a weekend of talking, shopping and fun. They went directly to the local mall and after enjoying a cappuccino, they went into a department store to pick up some new clothes for Susan to wear during the cold winter months ahead.

Claire said, "Let's start by picking out sweaters, so that you will have enough to keep warm.

Susan quickly found one she liked and exclaimed, "This one is really pretty, and I have lots of slacks to wear with it."

Claire said, "I'll hold onto the sweater and we can pick some more."

Susan quickly picked a couple more sweaters and Claire suggested that they move on to another part of the store to continue shopping. Susan stated, "Mom, I'm not sure I want this. I need to look more. These are just possibilities."

Frustrated Claire said, "Susan, I thought you said you wanted these. We can't spend all day just looking at sweaters!"

Susan replied sharply "Mom, you always want to take the fun out of shopping."

Claire responded angrily "I like to have fun the same as you, Susan. You never seem to be able to make up your mind." She further added, "And you're not very practical with many of your choices."

"What's not practical about my choice?" Susan asked. She took one of the sweaters that Claire was holding and exclaimed "There is nothing impractical about this sweater."

Claire replied, "Well the truth is that I don't like it. It is not a very cheerful color for you and it is not woven well on the waistline or sleeves. It looks cheap."

Susan said, " Mom…. I tried it on and looked in the mirror, and I think it looks good! I want it!"

"Tell me exactly what you can wear this with? Which slacks will you wear and what shirt can you wear under this? Why do you want to wear this thing?" Susan was silent.

The rest of the afternoon shopping was quiet and painful for them both.

***

Claire and Susan's conflict is based in the mental perception of their experience. Claire views her daughter as never being practical and failing to settle down and focus on one thing for very long. Susan feels that her mother is consistently prodding her for information that she does not have. Susan sees possibilities that do not have to have practical factual foundations. Her mother requires knowledge of what pieces will go with what before she accepts the possibility. Susan can see the sweater and know it will work, but her mother must have the concrete evidence to accept the fact.

Sunday after Church, Claire and Susan sat down with one of the Church counselors to talk about their conflict. The counselor discussed how perception takes two forms when it is processed in the mind. She explained that Claire has a preference for sensing and Susan prefers intuiting; both are normal and natural ways of integrating the information that we experience in our daily lives. As the counselor described the features of intuiting and how Susan will not typically focus upon the detailed facts about sweaters, but will have a big picture knowing of what will work, Claire began to understand the difference between her and her daughter. Susan admitted that sometimes the clothing that she buys does not work well and she will not wear it. The description by the counselor of the sensing preference helped Susan to see that her mother was not against her or trying to prove her incompetent. The counselor helped them to accept the differences and realize that the hurtful words that they used did not make sense given the natural differences. Claire admitted that sometimes Susan comes home with stuff that she can't imagine what it will look like, only to see it look really great when Susan puts it on. She had wondered how she knew it would look good. The understanding and acceptance that mother and daughter learned in this vignette resulted in a positive shift in their relationship. Shopping became more teamwork and Claire learned to simply ask if Susan was sure it would work. This caused Susan to take a second look that frequently stopped her from buying clothes to be donated to charity the following week.

T/F: Method for Judging and Deciding

Thinking ⬅━━━━━━━━━━━━━━━━━━⮕ **Feeling**

Making judgments and decisions is an everyday occurrence in life. Close personal dyads are frequently involved in decision-making processes. Unlike the perspective function of Sensing and iNtuiting, which is mostly irrational, the judgment function of Thinking and Feeling is easily within our ability to make choices as to which end we will use. Frustrations and hurt in close personal relationships occur when misattribution based upon a dyadic member's belief about the correct choice is violated by the other member's difference. When the choice is being made regarding an action that the dyadic members themselves will participate in, then both have a vested interest and may experience rejection during their decision/negotiation process.

You did what?

Ronald and Lucy have been married for nine months. They both have two weeks paid vacation and they have agreed to take one of the weeks of the vacation together in the Bahamas. Because it is cold where they live in Des Moines, Iowa, they thought that going to the Bahamas in January would help them to thaw out. One Friday afternoon Ron came home and announced to Lucy that he had booked the flights and hotel reservations and everything was all set for their vacation.

Lucy looked stunned and remarked, "You did what?"

Ronald sharply responded, "Well, I booked the flights and reservations that we talked about—our vacation in the Bahamas in January. You remember."

Lucy replied in an emotional tone, "You didn't even talk to me about it."

Ron responded, "We did talk about it and agreed to go in January. I researched and found that if we bought the tickets before the end of November, we could save a bundle, so I booked everything. What was there to talk about?"

Lucy said, "You always make decisions without me. You don't care about my feelings."

Ronald replied, "I was just making sure we had a good trip. I thought that was the best thing to do. I didn't know your feelings would be hurt. Besides, we always have to talk about everything. It doesn't make any sense. Sometimes we just need to do what is right and not talk about everything."

***

Lucy's concern with Ron's decision to book the vacation was not based on how well he did in flights, hotels and savings, but rather was from her belief that he deliberately chose not to include her in decisions regarding the details of the trip. Because her decision-making style is relational/ harmonious, she viewed Ron's behavior as a personal attack, indicating his lack of value for her opinion and input. Ron, whose preference is for logical outcome-based thinking decisions, was merely choosing what he believed was the most favorable outcome. He saw the process of booking the vacation as a challenge to make good choices and save the most money. He was unaware of his wife's love of the collaborative process and the belief that non-collaboration is either rejection or evidence of a control issue.

In subsequent counseling, when the couple became aware of their preferences for opposite polar ends of this dichotomy, they recognized the false attributions that each one held about the other's decision-making processes. Ron recognized that when it came to decisions involving both he and his wife that he needed to be certain to check whether she wished to be included in making the final decisions. Lucy became aware that she needed to be responsible and express directly to Ron when a decision was important for her so that he would be aware of her desires. Both admitted that they had begun to think of the other's decision-making style in pejorative terms, each seeing the other's preference for judgments as flawed and needing correction.

When there is an understanding of the judgment dichotomy, close personal relationships like Ron and Lucy's can develop strong bonds. This knowledge results in improving levels of acceptance and healing the pains of rejection that occurred through misattribution and ignorance. Including elements of both ends of the dichotomy of judgments in the decision-making process is possible for strong personal dyads when the value of both perspectives in the decision making process is understood and honored.

J/P: Method for Life Interaction/Orientation

Judging ◄—————————————► **Perception**

Our overt and covert expressed interactions in
life will directly impact those with whom we
have strong personal relationships. The joy of
experiencing life is vital to being healthy. How
we approach life, on a day-to-day or moment-
by-moment basis can be described in large part
by the J-P (Judgment / Perception) dichotomy.
The desire to enjoy life by making decisions and
judgments about how to live is in stark contrast
to simply perceiving life as it occurs. It is normal
to develop comfort with the method that we
employ. Frequently however, when our families
of origin consist of one way at the exclusion of
the other, we may learn to believe that the other
way of interacting with life is somehow flawed or
problematic.

Your life is messed up!!

Terry and Lindsay were close friends throughout
high school. They were excited about sharing a
college dorm room and getting to spend lots of
time together. At the beginning of the semester
everything was smooth with the usual late night
chatter and discussion regarding campus life
and academic experiences, but over time tension

began to arise in the dorm room. Lindsay's space was meticulously organized, the bed always made unless she was sleeping in it, all of her study materials put away on the desk in ordered stacks, and her clothes never in sight. Her personal belongings were never in the bathroom, and this is how she believed the entire dorm room was to be kept. Terry frequently crawled into bed with books still piled on the end that would sometimes slip on the floor and become obstacles over which one would have to step when traversing the dorm room floor at night. Terry functioned with a couple of rotating clothesbaskets, one dirty and one clean, out in the open at the foot of her bed. After a few weeks Lindsay began talking to Terry with gentle encouragement about how her organization made her side of the room look nice. Terry listened to her courteously but professed that she was not into that much wasting of time. Besides, they would only be in college once and she was not going to spend the time playing house. At the end of the first month communication had degraded to the point where Lindsay was complaining that she could not stand the pig sty and Terry was insisting that she had something wrong with her for wasting so much time while at college, simply organizing and structuring her little space.

Lindsay told Terry, "I think that there is something wrong with you if you want to live like this;

it's not right. Your space makes our room look like a pit."

Terry protested "Me? Something wrong with me? You're a neat freak and I think that there is something wrong with you! Your life is consumed with always cleaning and ordering. You're trying to make me be just like you, you're a control freak. You sound just like my mother."

Exasperated, Lindsay said, "You are simply lazy and I do not know how you ever expect to have a career or live with another human being."

After raising such a fuss that the floor supervisor heard them, they were both referred to student counseling services to see if they could develop more cooperation with each other or would need to be assigned to different rooms.

***

The issues that developed with Lindsay and Terry are very common in close personal relationships. Each one sees life differently and is happy with the way things are with themselves. Because of that comfort with their choices, whenever they are told that the way they live is wrong they defend by pointing out that the messenger is wrong. We like the way we live our lives. If we don't, we change it. Our time in our families of origin can solidify our comfort with our approach to life, and to be criticized for that choice may be interpreted as, we are bad. This is especially true when the message contains so many negative aspersions.

Lindsay and Terry patched up their relationship but agreed that they needed to switch roommates. While they understood their differences, they recognized that they could not be happy sharing that close of an environment together. They no longer say the negative things about each other and have both recognized that they would like to have more of the other's way of being for themselves. At the end of the semester they moved off campus into an apartment with the other two women who had become their new roommates. Decisions were made in agreement about the common space, but no one was to discuss another's private room condition. Acceptance led Lindsay and Terry to the freedom to compromise.

Acceptance
From Knowledge

Why do people struggle with individual differences? Why is there such a term as "Personality Conflict?" The answers to these questions lie in part in the natural process of acquisition of personal knowledge, but also in our own beliefs and feelings of being accepted. *Dichotomies for Dyads* was written to add to the body of information that is learned concerning natural personality characteristics. When we can understand the differences that we see in others as natural and healthy, then we are able to accept the differences without compromising our beliefs and values. This text describes what is natural and healthy and points out the common misattributions that occur when that information is absent.

Being accepted is the most powerful experience of life. It occurs at birth when our parents hold us and suspend all potential embarrassment by making funny faces and soft high-pitched sounds all in an attempt to let us know that we are welcomed, loved and enjoyed. As we develop and grow, our childhood errors provide us with opportunities to experience disapproval directed at us. We learn to discontinue our errors and negative behavior in order to stop the discomfort (from the disapproval) that those choices bring.

Unfortunately, as we get older the disapproval that we experience may arise as a response to our natural personality (not errors). This is not changeable. Yes, it is true we can act differently by choice, but our natural preference for other ways of being will leave some of us struggling to reconcile the chosen act from our preferred reality. Being wholly accepted for our natural personality selves frees us from confusion and the energy wasting stage production of being someone else.

Some people become chameleons and change personality as they change company. This frequently stems from early rejection of self that occurs shortly after experiencing the external rejection from one or more significant individuals (parent, school teacher or peers). The constant change of the contextual self in an effort to be accepted consumes the individual's psychological resources and results in personality type confusion. The boundaries between the core developed and contextual self are gone for this hurting individual. Context becomes core in a desperate effort to become accepted and loved. Exhaustive efforts can lead to bitterness and resentment over never being okay with their self and consequently others.

Self

Knowledge of our underlying innate personality type can bring about peace and stability within the self as the core identity is established and accepted.

By understanding your personality type and the natural differences that occur it then becomes possible or easier to accept dichotomously opposite others. There is no reason that we all cannot experience being valued and accepted without conforming to another's personality. Acceptance serves to halt the pain of rejection. Self-acceptance frees us to accept others.

The more we can learn about ourselves, the more clarity we have in our relationships, sorting out the misattributions from reality. There are many ways to gather information about personality. This text has focused upon personality typology, but there is also temperament theory, cognitive styles, interaction styles, and occupational tapestry. These can all add to our self and other understanding. For more information on these forms of personality investigation, go to 16types.com and sign up for a free account.

About the Author

DR. MARK S. MAJORS is a counseling
psychologist with extensive assessment develop-
ment experience that includes data analysis on
the 1994 Strong Interest Inventory, the MBTI®
Form M and Form Q, as well as the development of the IRT scoring for the MBTI® Form Q.
He was coauthor for the new MBTI® Form Q
Manual. Mark is also the author and developer
of the Majors Personality Type Inventory™
(MajorsPTI™), Majors Occupational Environment
Measure™ (MajorsOEM™), Majors Personality
Type-Elements™ (Majors PT-Elements™) and
co developer of the Interstrength® X-Styles
Assessment. In addition to being a test developer, Mark is president of a small private college
that specializes in training pastoral counselors
with an emphasis on the use of personality
assessment for conflict resolution through the

acceptance of differences and personal growth. He has provided sixteen years of successful individual and couples/marital counseling using the information contained in this text.

CPSIA information can be obtained at www.ICGtesting.com
Printed in the USA
LVOW062107200113

316480LV00001B/53/P